FRANCIS FRITH'S

TIVERTON PHOTOGRAPHIC MEMORIES

Trevor & Sue Southgate

16, Butterleigh Drive,

Tiverton,

Devon,

EX16 4PN

18th May 2012

THE FRANCIS FRITH COLLECTION

www.francisfrith.com

Photographic Memories

Francis Frith's
Around Tiverton

Dennis Needham

FRITH BOOK Co

Paperback edition published in the United Kingdom in 2000 by
The Francis Frith Collection

British Library Cataloguing in Publication Data

Francis Frith's Around Tiverton
Dennis Needham
ISBN 1-85937-178-7

The Francis Frith Collection
Frith's Barn, Teffont,
Salisbury, Wiltshire SP3 5QP
Tel: +44 (0) 1722 716 376
Email: info@francisfrith.co.uk
www.francisfrith.com

Printed and bound in Great Britain

Front Cover: Tiverton, Fore Street 1930 83210t

AS WITH ANY HISTORICAL DATABASE THE FRITH ARCHIVE IS CONSTANTLY BEING CORRECTED AND IMPROVED AND THE PUBLISHERS WOULD WELCOME INFORMATION ON OMISSIONS OR INACCURACIES

Contents

Francis Frith: *Victorian Pioneer*

FRANCIS FRITH, Victorian founder of the world-famous photographic archive, was a complex and multitudinous man. A devout Quaker and a highly successful Victorian businessman, he was both philosophic by nature and pioneering in outlook.

By 1855 Francis Frith had already established a wholesale grocery business in Liverpool, and sold it for the astonishing sum of £200,000, which is the equivalent today of over £15,000,000. Now a multi-millionaire, he was able to indulge his passion for travel. As a child he had pored over travel books written by early explorers, and his fancy and imagination had been stirred by family holidays to the sublime mountain regions of Wales and Scotland. 'What a land of spirit-stirring and enriching scenes and places!' he had written. He was to return to these scenes of grandeur in later years to 'recapture the thousands of vivid and tender memories', but with a different purpose. Now in his thirties, and captivated by the new science of photography, Frith set out on a series of pioneering journeys to the Nile regions that occupied him from 1856 until 1860.

Intrigue and Adventure

He took with him on his travels a specially-designed wicker carriage that acted as both dark-room and sleeping chamber. These far-flung journeys were packed with intrigue and adventure. In his life story, written when he was sixty-three, Frith tells of being held captive by bandits, and of fighting 'an awful midnight battle to the very point of surrender with a deadly pack of hungry, wild dogs'. Sporting flowing Arab costume, Frith arrived at Akaba by camel seventy years before Lawrence, where he encountered 'desert princes and rival sheikhs, blazing with jewel-hilted swords'.

During these extraordinary adventures he was assiduously exploring the desert regions bordering the Nile and patiently recording the antiquities and peoples with his camera. He was the first photographer to venture beyond the sixth cataract. Africa was still the mysterious 'Dark Continent', and Stanley and Livingstone's historic meeting was a decade into the future. The conditions for picture taking confound belief. He laboured for hours in his wicker dark-room in the sweltering heat of the desert, while the volatile chemicals fizzed dangerously in their trays. Often he was forced to work in remote tombs and caves where conditions were cooler. Back in London he exhibited his photographs and was 'rapturously cheered' by members of the Royal Society. His reputation as a photographer was made overnight. An eminent modern historian has likened their impact on the population of the time to that on our own generation of the first photographs taken on the surface of the moon.

Venture of a Life-Time

Characteristically, Frith quickly spotted the opportunity to create a new business as a specialist publisher of photographs. He lived in an era of immense and sometimes violent change. For the poor in the early part of Victoria's reign work was a drudge and the hours long, and people had precious little free time to enjoy themselves. Most had no transport other than a cart or gig at their disposal, and had not travelled far beyond the boundaries of their own town or village. However, by the 1870s, the railways had threaded their way across the country, and Bank Holidays and half-day Saturdays had been made obligatory by Act of Parliament. All of a sudden the ordinary working man and his family were able to enjoy days out and see a little more of the world.

With characteristic business acumen, Francis Frith foresaw that these new tourists would enjoy having souvenirs to commemorate their days out. In 1860 he married Mary Ann Rosling and set out with the intention of photographing every city, town and village in Britain. For the next thirty years he travelled the country by train and by pony and trap, producing fine photographs of seaside resorts and beauty spots that were keenly bought by millions of Victorians. These prints were painstakingly pasted into family albums and pored over during the dark nights of winter, rekindling precious memories of summer excursions.

The Rise of Frith & Co

Frith's studio was soon supplying retail shops all over the country. To meet the demand he gathered about him a small team of photographers, and published the work of independent artist-photographers of the calibre of Roger Fenton and Francis Bedford. In order to gain some understanding of the scale of Frith's business one only has to look at the catalogue issued by Frith & Co in 1886: it runs to some 670 pages, listing not only many thousands of views of the British Isles but also many photographs of most European countries, and China, Japan, the USA and

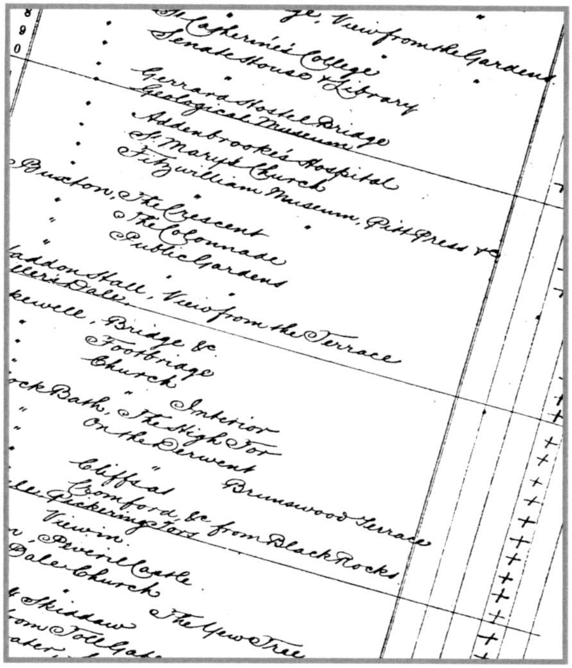

Canada – note the sample page shown above from the hand-written *Frith & Co* ledgers detailing pictures taken. By 1890 Frith had created the greatest specialist photographic publishing company in the world, with over 2,000 outlets – more than the combined number that Boots and WH Smith have today! The picture on the right shows the *Frith & Co* display board at Ingleton in the Yorkshire Dales. Beautifully constructed with mahogany frame and gilt inserts, it could display up to a dozen local scenes.

Postcard Bonanza

The ever-popular holiday postcard we know today took many years to develop. In 1870 the Post Office issued the first plain cards, with a pre-printed stamp on one face. In 1894 they allowed other publishers' cards to be sent through the mail with an attached adhesive halfpenny stamp. Demand grew rapidly, and in 1895 a new size of postcard was permitted called the court card, but there was little room for illustration. In 1899, a year after Frith's death, a new card measuring 5.5 x 3.5 inches became the standard format, but it was not until 1902 that the divided back came into being, with address and message on one face and a full-size illustration on the other. *Frith & Co* were in the vanguard of postcard development, and Frith's sons Eustace and Cyril continued their father's monumental task, expanding the number of views offered to the public and recording more and more places in Britain, as the coasts and countryside were opened up to mass travel.

Francis Frith died in 1898 at his villa in Cannes, his great project still growing. The archive he created continued in business for another seventy years. By 1970 it contained over a third of a million pictures of 7,000 cities, towns and villages. The massive photographic record Frith has left to us stands as a living monument to a special and very remarkable man.

Frith's Archive: *A Unique Legacy*

FRANCIS FRITH'S legacy to us today is of immense significance and value, for the magnificent archive of evocative photographs he created provides a unique record of change in 7,000 cities, towns and villages throughout Britain over a century and more. Frith and his fellow studio photographers revisited locations many times down the years to update their views, compiling for us an enthralling and colourful pageant of British life and character.

We tend to think of Frith's sepia views of Britain as nostalgic, for most of us use them to conjure up memories of places in our own lives with which we have family associations. It often makes us forget that to Francis Frith they were records of daily life as it was actually being lived in the cities, towns and villages of his day. The Victorian age was one of great and often bewildering change for ordinary people, and though the pictures evoke an impression of slower times, life was as busy and hectic as it is today.

We are fortunate that Frith was a photographer of the people, dedicated to recording the minutiae of everyday life. For it is this sheer wealth of visual data, the painstaking chronicle of changes in dress, transport, street layouts, buildings, housing, engineering and landscape that captivates us so much today. His remarkable images offer us a powerful link with the past and with the lives of our ancestors.

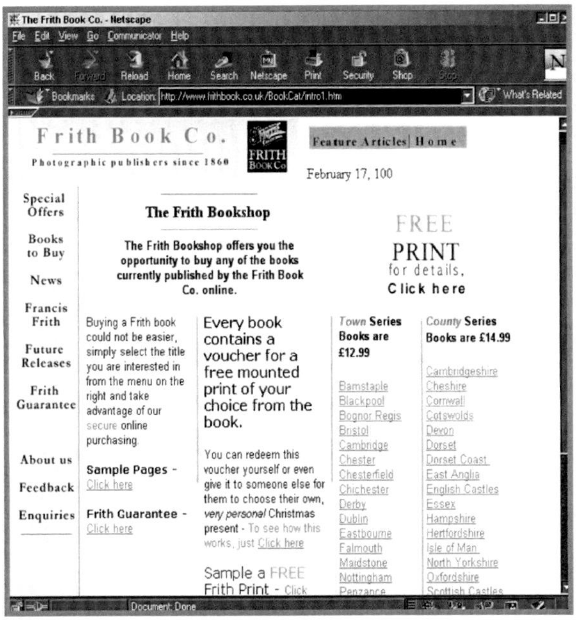

See Frith at www. frithbook.co.uk

Today's Technology

Computers have now made it possible for Frith's many thousands of images to be accessed almost instantly. In the Frith archive today, each photograph is carefully 'digitised' then stored on a CD Rom. Frith archivists can locate a single photograph amongst thousands within seconds. Views can be catalogued and sorted under a variety of categories of place and content to the immediate benefit of researchers.

Inexpensive reference prints can be created for them at the touch of a mouse button, and a wide range of books and other printed materials assembled and published for a wider, more general readership - in the next twelve months over a hundred Frith local history titles will be published! The day-to-day workings of the archive are very different from how they were in Francis Frith's time: imagine the herculean task of sorting through eleven tons of glass negatives as Frith had to do to locate a particular sequence of pictures! Yet the archive still prides itself on maintaining the same high standards of excellence laid down by Francis Frith, including the painstaking cataloguing and indexing of every view.

It is curious to reflect on how the internet now allows researchers in America and elsewhere greater instant access to the archive than Frith himself ever enjoyed. Many thousands of individual views can be called up on screen within seconds on one of the Frith internet sites, enabling people living continents away to revisit the streets of their ancestral home town, or view places in Britain where they have enjoyed holidays. Many overseas researchers welcome the chance to view special theme selections, such as transport, sports, costume and ancient monuments.

We are certain that Francis Frith would have heartily approved of these modern developments in imaging techniques, for he himself was always working at the very limits of Victorian photographic technology.

The Value of the Archive Today

Because of the benefits brought by the computer, Frith's images are increasingly studied by social historians, by researchers into genealogy and ancestory, by architects, town planners, and by teachers and schoolchildren involved in local history projects.

In addition, the archive offers every one of us an opportunity to examine the places where we and our families have lived and worked down the years. Highly successful in Frith's own era, the archive is now, a century and more on, entering a new phase of popularity.

The Past in Tune with the Future

Historians consider the Francis Frith Collection to be of prime national importance. It is the only archive of its kind remaining in private ownership and has been valued at a million pounds. However, this figure is now rapidly increasing as digital technology enables more and more people around the world to enjoy its benefits.

Francis Frith's archive is now housed in an historic timber barn in the beautiful village of Teffont in Wiltshire. Its founder would not recognize the archive office as it is today. In place of the many thousands of dusty boxes containing glass plate negatives and an all-pervading odour of photographic chemicals, there are now ranks of computer screens. He would be amazed to watch his images travelling round the world at unimaginable speeds through network and internet lines.

The archive's future is both bright and exciting. Francis Frith, with his unshakeable belief in making photographs available to the greatest number of people, would undoubtedly approve of what is being done today with his lifetime's work. His photographs, depicting our shared past, are now bringing pleasure and enlightenment to millions around the world a century and more after his death.

Tiverton - *An Introduction*

SITED AT THE confluence of the rivers Exe and Loman, Tiverton was founded in early Saxon times (probably around 650) and was originally known as Twyfyrde, literally 'double ford'. Not that this was the first sign of inhabitants in the area; Exeter Hill to the south has evidence of prehistoric earthworks.

Few records exist to tell of the town's development for the next few hundred years. The next detailed record of Tiverton is in 1106, when a large area of land was granted to one Richard de Redvers by Henry I. He built Tiverton Castle, which then became the family's residence. Richard's son Baldwin was created Earl of Devon. The fifth Earl managed to get Tiverton established as a borough around the start of the 13th century, but little happened until the manufacture of kersey began at the end of the 15th century. This is a coarse woollen cloth that became the basis for several fortunes to be earned in the town over the years. At that time, broad-cloth was the standard. It was heavy in weight and dark in colour, while kersey was lighter and dyed in bright reds, greens and blues. It was the increasing popularity of this type of cloth that made Tiverton what it is today. Wool from Devon sheep was generally coarse and unsuited to broad-cloth. However, it was perfect for kersey, and the woollen industry grew explosively.

As with many towns, Tiverton had its Great Fire. This destroyed much of the town in 1731. A few buildings were spared, one of them being a delightful merchants house in St Peter's Street. Not that this was the first fire either; two other serious ones occurred in 1598 and 1612.

Much of Tiverton's building comes as a direct result of the kersey trade. Peter Blundell, John Greenway, George Slee and John Waldron all made great fortunes; as was the way in those days, they bequeathed much for the improvement of the town. The latter three left us charming almshouses, whilst Peter Blundell gave us the school that carries his name.

His life was also a prime rags-to-riches story - as were those of the others, but perhaps to a lesser degree. Peter Blundell (1520-1601) started life as an errand boy for the town's kersey-makers. Saving what little he could, Peter eventually bought a roll of cloth for himself and got a friend to take it to London, where it was sold at a tidy profit. As is the way with people who make it to the top, he invested the proceeds in more cloth. His rapidly-burgeoning profits saw him soon established as both merchant and manufacturer. He was a benefactor of great note. Apart from Tiverton, hospitals in London and Exeter were grateful recipients of his wealth.

Did Peter Blundell have John Greenway as a rôle model? He was around when the first kersey boom was taking place. He was also a son of poor parents who had to make his own way in the world. His fortune came not only from being a wool merchant, but also from owning ships in which to carry his wares. These traded to the continent and carried fine wines back to this country on the return voyage. Greenway spent much of his later life in London where he was admitted to the Worshipful Company of the Drapers, a prestigious City guild. Pictures of his contribution to the town's architecture will be seen later.

Another important arrival in the town was John Heathcoat. He was a lace manufacturer from Leicestershire who suffered greatly at the hands of Luddites when he tried to introduce machinery to his factory. In Devon he found a more congenial climate, and his machines revolutionised lace production.

There have been many other notable names associated with the town. Henry John Temple was born in Westminster in 1784. In 1800 he inherited the family title and became the 3rd Viscount Palmerston. In 1835, as Lord Palmerston, he would become the town's MP; he served with distinction, becoming Prime Minister between 1855 and 1858 and again from 1859 to his death in 1865. He was an irascible man and was roundly disliked, but he was an excellent politician and a pragmatic judge of events. His most serious blunder was when he sold the warship 'Alabama' to the Confederacy during the American Civil War, thus siding with the rebels.

Derick Heathcote Amory was actually born in the town in 1899. He would later become MP for the town. Between 1958 and 1960 he served as Chancellor of the Exchequer in Harold Macmillan's government. He then became the 1st Viscount Amory and died in 1980.

As we will see later, the town is blessed with some distinguished religious buildings. St Peter's has the Greenway Chapel; more information about it will be discovered alongside the photographs. One lesser-known claim to fame is that the organ was used in 1847 at a wedding. Clearly, there is nothing unusual in that. But the music played was the March from Mendelssohn's 'Midsummer Night's Dream', and this was the first time that it was used for a wedding. Now, it is an almost indispensable part of every ceremony. Other churches also enhance the town. St George's in Fore Street is a perfect example of Georgian church architecture, and is the only one of its kind in Devon. The Baptist church in Newport Street is one of the oldest in the county; its roots are traceable to 1607.

As with many such rural towns, the coming of the railway made a real impact. From being a west country outpost, Tiverton was suddenly linked to the rest of the country. A station to the south on the main Great Western line between Bristol and Exeter was known as Tiverton Junction. Then a branch line was built into the town itself. This opened in 1848, and was a typical GWR branch service. Known locally as 'The Tivvy Bumper', it ran to and from the Junction to connect with main line services. There was also a line from Exeter along the Exe Valley directly into the town. This opened in 1885. From there, a line continued up the valley through Bampton to Morebath Junction, where it met the GWR line from Taunton to Barnstaple. Today, not a single piece of track is left. Even the Junction station on the main line has almost succumbed. The actual station has closed, but a new one was opened a short distance to the north known as Tiverton Parkway; there is a huge car park here, and travellers from all over north Devon gather here to catch their trains. The course of the railway through the town has disappeared under a new road, and the Tivvy Bumper never existed as far as people under the age of forty are concerned.

Fortunately for us, Francis Frith and his pioneering band of photographers did not confine their activities to the town alone. Realising that there were some simply wonderful villages in the surrounding countryside, they travelled the byways of the area searching out those special scenes which make this collection unique. And there is a wealth of interest and scenic beauty. One of the prettiest villages in this area must be Bickleigh. The thatched buildings create an aura of total pastoral charm. The bridge, which is featured in the photographs, is late 16th-century; it was damaged by floods in 1809 and had to be virtually rebuilt. The village is a short distance away from the water. More superb old buildings and St Mary's Church make this a place high on any tourist's must-see list.

Witheridge is an upland village, again established by the time of Domesday. The church here is a particular attraction. It has a square squat tower built of local dunstone; it is dedicated to St John the Baptist and is mainly 15th-century, restored in 1876. Visit Holcombe Rogus and admire a place where time has almost stood still. Acres of thatch and cob are to be seen too, so attractive and so characteristic of Devon.

One of the great pleasures of exploring both town and village is to carry this volume along with you. Enjoy the experience of working out just where our photographer set up his equipment all those years ago. As you snap away at the same view with your automatic focusing and winding camera, imagine the back-breaking load of equipment those pioneer photographers carried. Marvel at how little our green and pleasant land has changed during the intervening years. Or, perhaps, frown at the wanton destruction of eye-pleasing views by the architectural nightmares that sometimes stand in their place. Wonder at the acres of green fields that have disappeared under a welter of bricks and concrete.

This is a book for all seasons. Muse over it from your armchair during the long winter months. Then travel around during the more pleasant summer days. But above all, enjoy the sheer pleasure of nostalgia as displayed within these covers.

The Town

From Peffing's Howden 1890 23725
This is a vintage view of Tiverton as it was more than a century ago. Some of the buildings still gracing the town today can be seen. On the left is Heathcoat's Mill; the steeple is that of St Paul's, and the square tower is the parish church of St Peter. Towards the right, the railway to Exeter is just distinguishable.

General View 1930

83209

This photograph was taken from a hill to the south-east of town: it is possible to see some of the development that has taken place since the previous photograph. But the real beauty is beyond, as the hills of Exmoor start to dominate the scene.

The Lace Works 1890 23734

The Lace Works 1890
John Heathcoat was a local businessman who invented the bobbin net machine which revolutionised lace-making. This was his lace-making factory. Today, there is a thriving mill shop here, selling an extensive range of fabrics; it is very popular with seamstresses from miles around. It is housed in what was the factory school, which opened in 1841 and was the first in the west.

Leat Street Avenue 1914
This tree-lined street has no hint of development as yet. Note the road surface: although the footpaths appear to be made up and kerbs are in place, the road surface still bears the marks of cart wheels and is clearly not yet metalled.

Leat Street Avenue 1914 66527

St Paul's Street
1920 69889
This view is instantly recognisable today, with St Paul's Church at the head of the street. Mr Penny's emporium on the left has been demolished to improve the traffic flow.

▼ **The West Exe Recreation Park c1955** T55031
The park is still very popular with local residents; the attractive setting of West Exe Park was a pleasant milieu when this view was taken half a century ago, and has changed little in the intervening years.

▼ **The Paddling Pool c1960** T55034
The pool is just deep enough to get your feet wet. Paddling pools are still popular today, although their very nature leaves them open to vandalism. Several councils have given up the struggle and filled theirs in; not so in Tiverton.

▲ **The Playground c1960** T55035
Half a century ago, youngsters were satisfied with simple rides. Occasionally, they would fall off and run home with a bloody head. In today's more litigious age, local authorities choose their equipment with safety rather than fun in mind.

◄ **The New Council Houses c1955** T55015
After the last war, there was an explosion of new house building in Tiverton and many delightful old buildings were torn down. These new council houses are The Walronds, off Exeter Road.

St Andrew Street 1920

69892

This road was cut in half when a new by-pass was built round the town. This, the lower half, has changed somewhat, but mainly only in detail. To the extreme left was a public baths together with a police station and fire station.

◄ **The Town Hall 1890**
23726
This Italianate building was opened in 1864, and is used today by local councils and magistrates. It has changed little over the years. The building to the right has been demolished and replaced by a library. On the left is the elegant Georgian church of St George. It was built in Purbeck stone in 1730; the clock tower is now empty.

▼ **Little Silver 1914**
66530
The photographer appears to be quite the centre of attraction as the ladies from the left-hand house peer over the hedge. The youngsters on the extreme left coyly watch the camera, while the older ones seem more interested in how the photograph will be taken.

◄ **Old Cottages, Little Silver 1920** 69893
These houses in the Little Silver area would be worth a fortune today. Nestling at the foot of St Andrew Street, they were demolished after the last war when slum clearance was the watchword. Modernisation was embraced, and down everything came. What Hitler's bombers missed, the councils of England destroyed. What is built there today only emphasises the point.

◄ **Collipriest Walk 1914**
66526
It is clearly high summer and the horrors of World War One were still unknown to these two, even if not for long. They are obviously interested in something happening over the fence, down by the river.

Collipriest Avenue 1890 23735
This charming area is down the river from Little Silver, close to the confluence of the river Lowman. Today, the trees have grown appreciably, forming an almost impenetrable barrier. Upriver, on the left, the Tiverton railway line crosses the water on a bridge.

Collipriest Avenue 1914 66525
This road is actually alongside the Lowman, where tall trees create a charming walk for ladies of the town. Note the long dresses, still the height of fashion.

The Clock Tower and Lowman Bridge 1920 69890
This view is largely unchanged today. The building to the right of the clock tower is now Mallards Restaurant, and the next one along is still the Prince Regent. There is no evidence of motor vehicles, although horses are still in use: the stains on the road surface prove that. The statue is that of Edward VII, who reigned from 1901 to 1910.

The Clock Tower c1955 T55028
Viewed this time from Chapel Street, the river Lowman is seen here as a gentle stream. It can flood alarmingly, however, which is why a high wall behind the ramp, the flood alleviation scheme, has been built.

Greenway's Alms Houses 1896 38047
John Greenway was a merchant who will feature greatly in subsequent pages. His almshouses were a bequest in his will after his death in 1529. They were for five poor men who were allowed eight pence per week and had to pray for the soul of Greenway. The building in Gold Street pictured here is unchanged over a hundred years later.

Fore Street c1950 T55008
Much has changed since this view was captured, not least the fashions. The man to the right is wearing what was known as a demob suit: after military service, you were allowed a new suit. Cycles rather than cars dominate. The first two shops to the right, together with those on the left and the rather grand building at the end, are all demolished.

Gold Street 1903

49608

Our photographer is standing in the middle of Lowman Bridge to capture this view. To the extreme left, the bridge does not yet carry the statue of Edward VII. Thorne's Tea, Grocery and Provision Store on the right is a reminder of how we shopped in pre-supermarket days.

◄ **Castle Street 1920**

69888

This charming view is instantly recognisable today. The scooter, like the one to the left, is returning to fashion; perhaps children will once again sail yachts in the leat. It is sad that the leat normally carries no water today. It was installed back in 1250 as the town's water supply. The pub is still in business, but Mr Rudall, further along on the right, is not.

Gold Street c1950 T55007
We are looking down towards Lowman Bridge. The building with the car outside has become a branch of Specsavers; shaving was on offer next door, and the town's gasworks has gone.

The Castle, Old and New Parts 1896 38051
Tiverton Castle is a delightful amalgam of old and new. This view, taken from the rear and overlooking the river Exe, shows most of the new. The building is open to visitors on occasions, and regularly in high season.

The Castle, New Portion 1896 38052
This photograph was clearly taken at the same time as the previous one. It is intriguing that sun blinds now shield the window. Was this indicative of the length of time taken to set up a shot in those days? Note the croquet hoops on the lawn.

The Castle, Old Tower 1896 38055
Here we see some of the older parts of the building. The original castle was 12th-century; it was besieged by Parliamentarians during the Civil War. A lucky shot breached the drawbridge and the governor surrendered.

The Castle 1907 57454

The Castle 1914 66524

The Castle 1907
The ivy-covered walls of both old and new parts of the castle are clearly still well maintained. The site itself commands a superb view over the Exe Valley. Note the trees: this view was clearly taken in winter or spring.

The Castle 1914
In this view, taken just before the first world war, the undergrowth appears to be winning the battle. Part of the old tower is all that is visible here.

In the Park 1903

49612

The People's Park was opened in 1897 to mark Queen Victoria's golden jubilee, and it is still popular today. Many changes have taken place over the years. The Tivertonians seen in this view all appear to be smartly dressed; the fashionable perambulator is particularly worthy of note.

◄ **The Park 1920** 69897
The huge cannon which dominates this view has been removed, and the bandstand beyond it is no more. A bowling green, very popular with the locals, has replaced it.

◄ **The Park Entrance 1920** 69899
Children's wear apart, this view is unchanged save the removal of the trellis to the left-hand front of the house. Needless to say, the trees have also grown a little. The iron gates are still in place; they are a delightful ornament provided by our Victorian forefathers.

▼ **The Park 1920** 69896
This photograph gives a splendid impression of the delightful location of Tiverton. Looking west, the slopes of Exmoor are plain to see. In the valley immediately below, a new road is now a blot on the landscape.

◄ **The Park 1920** 69898
Three young ladies, together with their doll's pram, sit in front of a statue which still adorns the People's Park. Their outfits - and those to the left as well - are very much in keeping with the times.

◄ **Swinesbridge 1920**

69903

This is a similar view to the photograph above. Again, progress has destroyed much of it.

Penny Park 1930
83223
At this time, views such as these could be replicated a hundred times throughout the county of Devon. Thatch, unsurfaced road and total absence of traffic was the norm. Today, most of these views have gone.

Knightshayes Court 1896 38057
Now owned by the National Trust, this building was begun in 1869; it is a rare example of the architecture of William Burges. The owners, the Heathcoat-Amery family, have been (and still are) active in both national and local politics.

A Country View c1960
T55045
Close to Tiverton, this could be said to be archetypal Devon: rolling hills, cultivated fields and a small farm tucked away from the world. The communications revolution may have hit Devon, but views like this can still be found quite easily.

Watery Tiverton

The River Exe from the Bridge 1890 23738
The tower of St Peter's church overlooks the Exe as it flows through Tiverton. Again, this is a timeless view, although the bank to the left has been campshedded to alleviate the flooding problems that were endemic to Tiverton once upon a time.

▼ **The River Exe from the Bridge 1890** 23737
The main course of the river Exe is to the right. The lesser course, arriving from the left, was a leat dug to serve Heathcoat's mill. The photograph is taken from the town bridge, once the only crossing of the Exe in town.

▼ **The River Exe 1920** 69894
This view was taken from the town bridge, with much of the tree growth seen in earlier photographs cut down. The buildings revealed are almost identical to those which the Tiverton visitor can see today.

▲ **Lowman Bridge 1920** 69891
The Clock Tower was a gift to the town by Thomas Ford, who lived locally. He was also responsible for the statue of Edward VII. The tree in the centre of the photograph has been replaced by a set of toilets.

◄ **The King Edward Statue and the Bridge c1955**

T55029

This is another view of Lowman Bridge with its statue. The building to the right is 17th-century; it has recently been converted to a delightful hotel and restaurant.

The River Exe and Collipriest House 1890 23736
Below the town, Collypriest House is one of the better residences in town. It is an elegant Georgian mansion which is not open to visitors. It was once the residence of the Blundell family. The only change today from this view over a century ago is that a television aerial has been added.

◄ **Washfield, The Weir 1920** 69904
Although the Exe is a natural watercourse, it is also used as a conduit to bring water to both Tiverton and Exeter. To this end, a large reservoir at Wimbleball, north of Bampton, ensures that the supply of water is constant.

◄ **The Weir c1955** T55023
Upstream of Tiverton, there are several weirs on the river Exe as it plunges down from Exmoor. The river rises high in these hills, but only a few miles from the Bristol Channel. It is remarkable that instead of running that way, it picks its way across Devon for 55 miles before emptying into the English Channel at Exmouth.

▼ **Washfield, The Weir 1920** 69906
For many years, salmon were an important catch in the river. They still run today, but in nothing like the quantities they once did. At some of the weirs, salmon ladders have been provided to help them ascend to their spawning grounds.

◄ **On the Canal 1903** 49613
The Grand Western Canal was part of a grandiose scheme to link the Bristol and English Channels between Taunton and Exeter. There were to be three branches, one of which was Tiverton. This view, at Tidcombe Bridge, shows the canal in a near-derelict state.

The Grand Western Canal 1930 83225

The section between Lowdwells and Tiverton was built for barges and survives today. From Lowdwells to Taunton, the canal could only accommodate boats that carried only six tons; this was hopelessly uneconomical as soon as the railways arrived.

The Canal c1955 T55022

Barges had continued to carry limestone from a quarry at Westleigh to lime kilns in Tiverton Basin. This trade lasted until 1924, when the whole canal was closed but never infilled. In 1971, Devon council took over the canal from British Waterways and have retained it as a leisure amenity ever since.

The Canal c1955 T55021
This is one of the many accommodation bridges which cross the canal. Today, this is all beautifully restored. There is an excursion boat operating from Tiverton Basin which is horse-drawn. This makes a stunningly beautiful trip.

School & Church

St Peter's Church c1890 T55501
The doorway in the north aisle is all that remains of the Norman church that was consecrated by Bishop Leofric in 1073. Most of today's building dates from 1412 to 1429, although there have been several subsequent attempts at restoration. Of particular interest are the kneelers, which have been made by members of the church over the last forty years; the local scenes are delightful examples of the embroiderers' craft.

◄ **St Peter's Church, The Greenway Chapel and Porch c1960**

T55062

Much of the carving depicts the life of Greenway. He was a poor boy who grew to become a prominent cloth merchant. He was a member of the Worshipful Company of Drapers and the Merchant Venturers of London.

St Peter's Church, The Greenway Chapel 1890 23732
One of the most astonishing parts of this building is the Greenway Chapel. This was built by John Greenway (whom we met earlier in the introduction) in 1517, and is simply dazzling, even 450 years later.

S. Peter's Church, The Greenway Chapel, 16th-Century Armed Merchantmen c1960 T55063
As a ship owner, Greenway had each of his fleet illustrated here. This one can be seen on the buttress to the right of the south door. Note the gun ports: in those days, substantial defence was needed against pirates.

St Peter's Church, The Organ c1960 T55066
This beautiful instrument was installed in 1696 after strong opposition from the more Calvinist branch of the church. The builder was Bernard Schmidt, organist to King William III. It was completely rebuilt in 1867, but much of the original case and many of the pipes were re-used.

St Peter's Church, The Lion and the Unicorn c1960 T55067
The mayor's pew is guarded by these ornately-carved figures. They probably date back to 1615 when Tiverton received its Charter.

Blundell's Old School 1903 49610

This is the entrance to the original Blundell's School - Old Blundell's. This was built in 1604 by Peter Blundell; it continued to educate the children of gentlemen until 1882, when a new school was opened further out of town.

Blundell's Old School 1921 69895
After the old school's closure, the building was sold, but trustees collected funds from old Blundellians and the building was re-purchased in 1940 and handed to the school's governors in 1945. In 1954 they gave it to the National Trust, who manage it today. The grounds are open, but not the building.

Blundell's New School 1890 23733
Only a few years after removal to this site, the new school building was in place. But it was not quite complete. For instance, the hole at the top of the tower was left to allow a clock to be fitted.

▲ **Blundell's School 1896** 38048
Six years after the photograph on the previous page, the clock was in place. The chapel tower to the left of this picture is still extant, but, as we will see later, it will be demolished.

◄ **Blundell's School 1920** 69900
It is a quarter of a century after the above photograph , and there is absolutely no change to note - apart from the vehicle, that is.

▲ **Blundell's School from the Playing Field 1930** 83213
The spire mentioned earlier, and still visible in 1920, is now no more; it has been replaced by a square tower. This view shows the extensive playing fields - sports have always had a strong tradition here.

◄ **Blundell's School, the Chapel and the War Memorial 1930** 83216
The extended school chapel and the new tower are much more prominent in this view. Some of England's better-known characters call Blundell's their alma mater. R D Blackmore, who wrote 'Lorna Doone', was educated here; he set the opening scenes of his book in the school. Jack Russell, the hunting parson and dog breeder, and Samuel Wesley, brother of John, were also pupils here.

Blundell's School Chapel 1930 83218
The school is still an integral part of Tiverton life; out of school hours, the roads here are crowded with (generally) well-behaved pupils enjoying the town. Both boarders and day pupils are accommodated.

Blundell's School Chapel, Interior 1930 83219
This glorious piece of architecture almost seems wasted on a school chapel. The pupils treat it with due reverence, and Old Blundellians remember it with affection. This view shows a screen that had disappeared by the 1950s.

Blundell's School Chapel, Interior 1930 83221
After he had taken the previous photograph, our cameraman turned right round and took this view, looking to the rear of the building. To this day, pupils of this popular private school crowd through the doors for services.

◄ **Bradninch, The Guildhall 1870**
B386002
Over a century and a quarter along, this view is essentially unchanged. Both pub and Guildhall still exist, and have been subjected to only cosmetic changes. The policeman's uniform and the other clothing have also undergone something of a change. On the extreme left, a gentleman is still wearing a stovepipe hat. The gun was captured at Sebastopol.

The Surrounding Areas

◄ **Upton Hellions**
The Church c1965
U57047
This tiny church is in a typical Devonian hamlet. The solidly-built square tower seems almost too big for the body of the building. A father and son stroll nonchalantly past the cameraman.

▼ **Bradninch, Fore Street c1965** B386301
The cars have altered (and there are considerably more of them), the trees have grown somewhat, and the telephone poles have disappeared. Otherwise, this is an instantly recognisable view.

◄ **Cheriton Fitzpaine, The Village c1955**
C305004
This is a charming Devonian village with its pub, the Ring of Bells. Note the neatness and quality of the thatch. Many buildings in this area still use this material for their roofs.

▼ **Cheriton Fitzpaine, General View c1955** C305010
As mentioned in the caption to photograph No C305004, thatch is still common in this area. A study of this view will confirm that fact.

▼ **Bickleigh, The River and the New Inn 1930** 83230
The narrow road was just about suitable for the volume of traffic when this view was taken. Today, it is hardly at all wider, and the traffic is horrendous; this is not surprising in such a wonderful location. The New Inn is now the Trout Inn; it still has a thatched sign.

▲ **Bickleigh, The River 1930** 83231
This view of the riverside was taken from Bickleigh Bridge. The lowering skies are clearly standard English holiday weather; the cameraman is having to fight his eternal battle against bad light.

◄ **Bickleigh, The River 1930** 83233
Here we see Tea Cottage, as it was known at the time. Today, it has become Bickleigh Cottage Hotel, but it still looks as pretty as it did then.

Bickleigh, The Bridge and the River Exe 1930 83235
Hopelessly inadequate for today's traffic levels, the bridge (with no footpath) can manage vehicles in one direction only. Despite that, it is still quite majestic. Our photographer seems to have left his carrying bag in shot, down in the bottom left corner.

◄ **Bickleigh, The River 1930** 83234

This is an idyllic riverside view as the Exe flows gently through the edge of Bickleigh. The village is set back some distance from the water, and is a pure heaven of cob walls and thatch.

▼ **Bickleigh Fishermen's Cottages 1934** 86223

This assortment of buildings in a most gorgeous setting appear to be as meticulously maintained in this view as they are today. The river Exe is a noted fishing river.

◄ **Bickleigh The Fisherman's Cot c1960** B84004

This building is still the same today, a mass of thatch and low ceilings. The pub is open most days all day; it serves excellent food as well as some good real ales. An extensive car park is often full to capacity at weekends.

MARFAK

Witheridge, Fore Street c1960 W574005
All has changed here since 1960. On the left, the garage is out of business, but the white building stands, albeit with the garage doors infilled. Beyond, everything has been destroyed. Electricity poles still carry supplies to the village. There is a thatcher at work on the right-hand side in the far distance.

Witheridge, The Square c1960 W574018
Two lovely old AEC buses from Devon General await customers in the Square. The shop on the extreme left is still a post office, but the gabled building behind the right-hand bus is no more. On the extreme right is an empty space.

Witheridge, The Village c1965 W574031
The empty space we saw in the previous photograph is, five years later, occupied by a toilet. The centre part of this building, a bus shelter then, is now converted to a disabled toilet. Otherwise, this sleepy little village has let the years pass by with little change.

Culmstock, General View c1960 C312312
In fairness, Culmstock is not one of England's natural tourist attractions. But there are better corners than can be seen from this view. The church, for instance, is 15th-century and is built of local flint. This view is taken from the tower.

Culmstock, The Beacon c1960 C312309
The church tower is not the only vantage point in the area. Culmstock Beacon is a mile to the north of town, and stands almost 800ft above sea level. It once offered a wonderful view over towards the Blackdown Hills as well as Exmoor. Now, the M5 motorway tears along at its foot.

▼ **Holcombe Rogus, The Village from the Church Tower c1960** H243022
We are overlooking the village, with the hills in the background where Culmstock Beacon sits. The church (All Saints) is 15th-century and offers a splendid view over this most attractive village

▼ **Holcombe Rogus, Waterloo Stores c1960** H243009
The village store in Holcombe Rogus is consigned to the history books, although a local garage now sells some of the items offered here. The tobacco advertising is quite amazing to our 21st-century eyes: Players, Bachelor, Woodbine, Park Drive and Bristol cigarettes are mentioned. A chocolate machine sits on the wall. The building today is a private dwelling, Waterloo House.

▲ **Holcombe Rogus**
The House c1960
H243015
Next door to the church is this delightful Tudor mansion, built in the mid 1500s. Since then, there has been much addition to it, but the integrity of the old building has not been compromised. It is privately owned and not open to visitors.

◄ **Holcombe Rogus, Ford House c1960** H243048
Ford House, opposite a large pond, had a pack of hounds being exercised alongside as the cameraman visited. How long this evocative sight will be allowed to continue is a moot point.

Sampford Peverell, The Globe Hotel c1960 S355006
A remarkable transformation has taken place here. The old render has been removed, and the building is now stone-faced and looks quite delightful. Starkey's Tivvy Ales are no more (inevitably), but there are several good real ales always on offer. The buildings beyond the pub have disappeared.

Sampford Peverell, Boobery c1960 S355011
This is a quiet corner of a quiet village. The scene is difficult to see today because of the massive growth of trees and bushes all around. It is still glorious Devon at its glorious best, though.

Halberton, The Village 1930 83224
The village pond, down by the church, is still a central attraction to villagers, as it was then. The clothing worn by children today has altered more than somewhat. The terrace of houses above the pond has been replaced by newer buildings.

Halberton
The Village 1930
83228
After the cameraman took the previous photograph, he walked past the pond and turned round to photograph this view. The pond is now on the right, and the 14th-century tower of St Andrew's Church is plain to see.

Halberton
The Village 1930

83229

A crowd awaits the next bus into Tiverton as a youngster is fascinated by our cameraman. The New Inn is now known as the Barge (the Grand Western Canal comes through the village). The signpost in front of the pub is still in place and carries the legend 'Welcome Inn'. Take your pick!

Chettiscombe, The Village 1930 83227
Three walkers lounge on the bridge by the ford in Chettiscombe. There is an intriguing feature to the left of the camera: this is the Town Leat that once supplied Tiverton with its water.

Chettiscombe, The Village 1930 83226
We are a few yards downstream from the view pictured above, and the people on the bridge have been replaced by a lady. There is a horse-drawn farm implement to the right of shot. Chettiscombe is a most ancient place, being mentioned in Domesday.

Bampton, The Railway c1955 B379040
A Great Western class 4575 Prairie (2-6-2 wheel arrangement) loco starts the climb towards Bampton with a train from Tiverton to Morebath Junction. Although overgrown, the view is still available. It was taken at the junction of the A396 and the B3190 by the Exeter Inn, a mile south of Bampton.

Bampton, The Chain Bridge c1955 B379014
This sturdy structure still crosses the river Exe about a mile along the A396 from where the previous photograph was taken. There is a charming thatched cottage guarding the bridge.

Bampton, Oakford Bridge, the Exe Valley c1955 B379034
This tiny little bridge is on a tiny back-road that sees little traffic today. At the time of this photograph, the bridge had recently undergone repairs following damage during the cloudburst higher up on Exmoor that was responsible for the Lynmouth flood disaster.

Bampton, The White Horse Hotel c1955 B379013
This was once an important stopping place on the main road from Taunton to the north Devon area; now, a new road further south has removed much of the traffic from this place. The pub has lost its porch and the horse above it, but the early 14th-century tower of St Michael's still stands over the town.

Bampton
Castle Street c1955 B379023
An indication of why a relief road was vital to Bampton can be seen from this view looking down into the town centre. The pub on the left is still open, but it has no sign on the wall; the filling station is now a private house, and the cafe behind has gone.

The interior of a derelict cell, 1977

The police station in 1872

HISTORIC MID DEVON:

Life Behind Bars

This month we look back at how criminals were dealt with in the area, where they were housed and in some cases, where they escaped…

The south end of Tiverton's St. Andrew Street contains a striking building which was once the Borough Gaol. It was built in 1846, designed by local architect Gideon Acland Boyce. Originally, the building contained the Governor's House and the gaol, including wings for men, women and debtors which could house 35 people. It was used to house people serving short sentences.

In 1855 the cells were described as containing 'a bright metal wash basin, tap for the supply of water, water closet, hammock, mattress and bedding, bible and prayer book; a bell which, when rung, causes a small iron plate, with the cell number, to project into the passage for the guidance of the officer on duty. There is a neat chapel where the prisoners have separate boxes, and if desirable, cannot even see each other.' This description also tells us that there were four cells in the basement, one for 'dark punishment' and three for vagrants who were committed for short periods.

This wasn't Tiverton's first gaol building. In 1630 Richard Hill (also known as Spurway) gave or sold to the town a house built on the site of the old St. Andrew chapel on the condition that it was used as a house of correction. This was later rebuilt around 1780, but wasn't very sturdy as nine prisoners escaped in 1842 by breaking through the walls (probably made of cob) with a small chisel.

In his book 'The Chronicles of Twyford', Snell records that Tiverton was called 'Old Whipshire' on account of culprits being whipped from the Bridewell up the street and round town. By 1828 the county gaol in Exeter would take 10 prisoners a year to work the treadmill there, whilst those left in Tiverton would continue to beat hemp or break road stone. People convicted of more 'serious' crimes (such as stealing a watch) would be transported to Australia.

The Governor's House part of the building became the town's police station, probably around 1860 when the new Town Hall was built. The gaol closed in 1878 when all prisoners were henceforth sent to Exeter gaol. The Police Station remained until 1956 when it relocated to Beechwood on The Avenue. The old gaol building had various uses after this, including a Civil Defence store, a youth centre and Dr Nicholson's surgery. The gaol was demolished in the 1970s, and the police station has been converted into housing.

TIVERTON MUSEUM of Mid Devon Life

This story and many others will be shared at an exhibition at Tiverton Museum this Autumn. Date is to be confirmed. For more information and for a finalised date, visit. ***www.tivertonmuseum.org.uk***

Big Ideas for Little Ones:
STAYCATION STAYCATION STAYCATION

Pre-2020, you could be forgiven for thinking that 'Lockdown' was perhaps the title of the latest hit by Stormzy or Skepta – but now, we're in no doubt; lockdown is no party. You've survived months of confinement in your homes – HUGE pat on the back to you all, seriously – but now you're probably wondering how you're going to survive the summer holidays. Don't worry, we've got you covered...

Usually, the summer holidays for us would include a holiday, maybe to see my family in Cyprus, or a camping trip, either of which would break up the 6-week stint off school. This year, like many, we are planning a staycation – all the perks of a holiday, but with the comfort of your own bed and loo!

Here's a few ideas to keep everyone entertained during this year's socially distanced summer holidays:

1 Pitch up

Across the country, hotels and camp sites are opening up for business again, so why not visit somewhere you've never been before? It's a great opportunity to explore the parts of Blighty you've always wanted to. If you don't feel confident staying away from home just yet, why not pitch a tent in your back garden and have a weekend sleeping under the stars? The children will love it and you get to have a hot shower without queuing – winner!

2 Takeaway Treats

When Edward was tiny, we stayed away in Padstow for a week and as we didn't want to eat out every night juggling a small baby, we planned a week of takeaways and meal deals in the comfort of our accommodation. You could easily do the same in a holiday rental or at home – the beauty of a 'Two Can Dine for £X' deal is that there is minimal cooking and hardly any washing up, and a takeaway is even less effort and just as much of a treat. A great way to give yourself a week off from cooking.

3 Themed Fun

Have a theme day at home; just pick a theme that the whole family love and then plan activities around that at home. For example, you could choose 'Wild Animals', and everyone could dress up as their favourite and have a jungle themed

Index

FRITH PRODUCTS & SERVICES

Francis Frith would doubtless be pleased to know that the pioneering publishing venture he started in 1860 still continues today. Over a hundred and forty years later, The Francis Frith Collection continues in the same innovative tradition and is now one of the foremost publishers of vintage photographs in the world. Some of the current activities include:

INTERIOR DECORATION

Today Frith's photographs can be seen framed and as giant wall murals in thousands of pubs, restaurants, hotels, banks, retail stores and other public buildings throughout the country. In every case they enhance the unique local atmosphere of the places they depict and provide reminders of gentler days in an increasingly busy and frenetic world.

PRODUCT PROMOTIONS

Frith products are used by many major companies to promote the sales of their own products or to reinforce their own history and heritage. Frith promotions have been used by Hovis bread, Courage beers, Scots Porage Oats, Colman's mustard, Cadbury's foods, Mellow Birds coffee, Dunhill pipe tobacco, Guinness, and Bulmer's Cider.

GENEALOGY AND FAMILY HISTORY

As the interest in family history and roots grows world-wide, more and more people are turning to Frith's photographs of Great Britain for images of the towns, villages and streets where their ancestors lived; and, of course, photographs of the churches and chapels where their ancestors were christened, married and buried are an essential part of every genealogy tree and family album.

FRITH PRODUCTS

All Frith photographs are available Framed or just as Mounted Prints and Posters (size 23 x 16 inches). These may be ordered from the address below. Other products available are - Address Books, Calendars, Jigsaws, Canvas Prints, Postcards and local and prestige books.

THE INTERNET

Already ninety thousand Frith photographs can be viewed and purchased on the internet through the Frith websites and a myriad of partner sites.

For more detailed information on Frith products, look at this site:
www.francisfrith.com

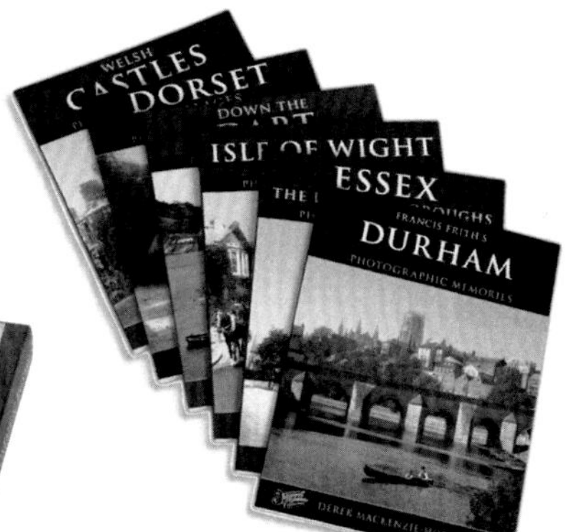

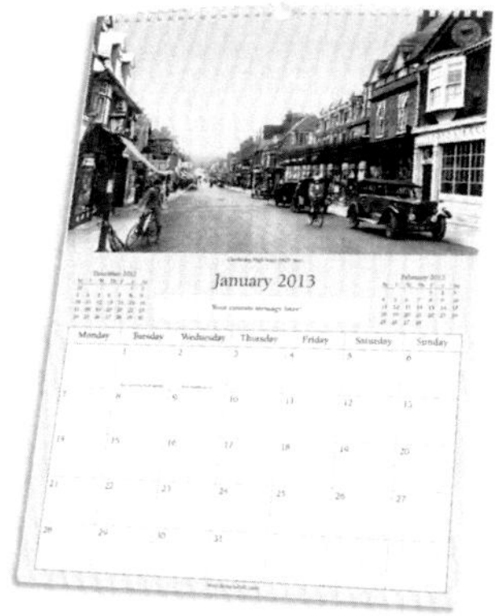

See the complete list of Frith Books at: www.francisfrith.com
This web site is regularly updated with the latest list of publications from The Francis Frith Collection. If you wish to buy books relating to another part of the country that your local bookshop does not stock, you may purchase on-line.

For further information, trade, or author enquiries please contact us at the address below:
The Francis Frith Collection, Unit 6, Oakley Business Park, Wylye Road, Dinton, Wiltshire SP3 5EU.
Tel: +44 (0)1722 716 376 Fax: +44 (0)1722 716 881 Email: sales@francisfrith.co.uk

See Frith products on the internet at www.francisfrith.com

FREE PRINT OF YOUR CHOICE

Mounted Print
Overall size 14 x 11 inches (355 x 280mm)

Choose any Frith photograph in this book. Simply complete the Voucher opposite and return it with your remittance for £3.50 (to cover postage and handling) and we will print the photograph of your choice in SEPIA (size 11 x 8 inches) and supply it in a cream mount with a burgundy rule line (overall size 14 x 11 inches). **Please note: aerial photographs and photographs with a reference number starting with a "Z" are not Frith photographs and cannot be supplied under this offer. Offer valid for delivery to one UK address only.**

***PLUS:* Order additional Mounted Prints at HALF PRICE - £10.00 each** (normally £20.00)
If you would like to order more Frith prints from this book, possibly as gifts for friends and family, you can buy them at half price (with no additional postage and handling costs).

***PLUS:* Have your Mounted Prints framed**
For an extra £19.00 per print you can have your mounted print(s) framed in an elegant polished wood and gilt moulding, overall size 16 x 13 inches (no additional postage and handling required).

IMPORTANT!

These special prices are only available if you use this form to order. You must use the ORIGINAL VOUCHER on this page (no copies permitted). We can only despatch to one UK address. This offer cannot be combined with any other offer.

Send completed Voucher form to:
The Francis Frith Collection, Unit 6, Oakley Business Park, Wylye Road, Dinton, Wiltshire SP3 5EU

CHOOSE A PHOTOGRAPH FROM THIS BOOK

Voucher *for FREE and Reduced Price Frith Prints*

Please do not photocopy this voucher. Only the original is valid, so please fill it in, cut it out and return it to us with your order.

Picture ref no	Page no	Qty	Mounted @ £10.00	Framed + £19.00	Total Cost £
		1	Free of charge*	£	£
			£10.00	£	£
			£10.00	£	£
			£10.00	£	£
			£10.00	£	£
			£10.00	£	£
			* Post & handling		£3.50
			Total Order Cost		£

Please allow 28 days for delivery.
Offer available to one UK address only

Title of this book ....

I enclose a cheque/postal order for £ ....
made payable to 'The Francis Frith Collection'

OR please debit my Mastercard / Visa / Maestro card, details below

Card Number:

Issue No (Maestro only): Valid from (Maestro):

Card Security Number: Expires:

Signature:

Name Mr/Mrs/Ms ....

Address ....

....

....

.... Postcode ....

Daytime Tel No ....

Email ....

Valid to 31/12/14

Free Print - see overleaf

Can you help us with information about any of the Frith photographs in this book?

We are gradually compiling an historical record for each of the photographs in the Frith archive. It is always fascinating to find out the names of the people shown in the pictures, as well as insights into the shops, buildings and other features depicted.

If you recognize anyone in the photographs in this book, or if you have information not already included in the author's caption, do let us know. We would love to hear from you, and will try to publish it in future books or articles.

An Invitation from The Francis Frith Collection to Share Your Memories

The 'Share Your Memories' feature of our website allows members of the public to add personal memories relating to the places featured in our photographs, or comment on others already added. Seeing a place from your past can rekindle forgotten or long held memories. Why not visit the website, find photographs of places you know well and add YOUR story for others to read and enjoy? We would love to hear from you!

www.francisfrith.com/memories

Our production team

Frith books are produced by a small dedicated team at offices near Salisbury. Most have worked with the Frith Collection for many years. All have in common one quality: they have a passion for the Frith Collection.

Frith Books and Gifts

We have a wide range of books and gifts available on our website utilising our photographic archive, many of which can be individually personalised.

www.francisfrith.com

Contains material sourced from responsibly managed forests.

FF006150